WATERPOCKET FOLD

HENRY MOUNTAINS

GOOD HOPE MESA

THE RINCON

MANCOS MESA

LONG CANYON

HALLS CROSSING

SHOCK TRAIL

RINCON

GLEN CANYON

SAN JUAN RIVER

DIRTY DEVIL RIVER

COLORADO RIVER

MILES

5   0   5   10

1963

MILDRED SOPHIE PORTER

IN THE PLACE NO ONE KNEW

THE PLACE NO ONE KNEW

On the walls, and back many miles into the country, numbers of monument-shaped buttes are observed. So we have a curious ensemble of wonderful features—carved walls, royal arches, glens, alcove gulches, mounds, and monuments. From which of these features shall we select a name? We decided to call it Glen Canyon.

—JOHN WESLEY POWELL, 1869

1. Wall and river's edge

Past these towering monuments, past these mounded billows of orange sandstone,

past these oak-set glens, past these fern-decked alcoves, past these mural

curves, we glide hour after hour, stopping now and then, as our attention is

arrested by some new wonder.—JOHN WESLEY POWELL, 1869

by ELIOT PORTER

THE PLACE

NO ONE KNEW

EDITED BY DAVID BROWER

Glen Canyon on the Colorado

Sierra Club · San Francisco

Publisher's Note: Glen Canyon is lithographed in four colors on one-sided Kromekote and lacquered to achieve maximum brilliance and fidelity in the color reproductions, themselves made directly from 4 x 5 and 2¼ x 2¼ transparencies. The text is on the uncalendered side for easier reading. The pages had to be collated singly and side-sewn; this assures a firm anchorage, among other advantages, but prevents the book's lying quite flat—especially the left-hand pages. The color, however, is the main thing to display.

It was of transcending importance to have a top-quality printer who would hue to Mr. Porter's interpretation. Barnes Press, Inc., New York City, met the platemaking and printing challenge just as the firm had done for Eliot Porter's earlier book, *"In Wildness . . ."* The book is set in Centaur and Arrighi by Mackenzie & Harris, Inc., San Francisco. It is bound in Columbia Mills' Sampson linen by Sendor Bindery, New York City. The design is by David Brower.

We are grateful for permission to reprint excerpts from these books:

Atheneum Publishers, New York: *The Firmament of Time,* by Loren Eiseley, copyright 1960 by Loren Eiseley.
Duell, Sloan & Pearce, New York: *Mormon Country,* by Wallace Stegner. Copyright 1942.
Harper & Row, New York: *Of Men and Mountains,* by William O. Douglas, copyright 1950; *Traveler in the Wilderness,* by Cid Ricketts Sumner, copyright 1957; *The Mind as Nature,* by Loren Eiseley, copyright 1962.
Holt, Rinehart and Winston, Inc., New York: *The Colorado,* by Frank Waters, copyright 1946.
Houghton Mifflin Company, Boston: *Beyond the Hundredth Meridian,* by Wallace Stegner, copyright 1954.
Alfred A. Knopf, Inc., New York: *Science in the Cause of Man,* by Gerard Piel, copyright 1961.
Little, Brown & Company—Atlantic Monthly Press, Boston: *In Friendly Candor,* by Edward Weeks, copyright 1946, 1947, 1951, 1955, 1956, 1957, 1958, 1959 by Edward Weeks.
Oxford University Press, Inc., New York: *A Sand County Almanac, and Sketches Here and There,* by Aldo Leopold, copyright 1949.
Random House, Inc., New York: *The Immense Journey,* by Loren Eiseley, copyright 1957.
William Sloane Associates, New York: *The Voice of the Desert,* by Joseph Wood Krutch, copyright 1956; *Grand Canyon,* by Joseph Wood Krutch, copyright 1957, 1958 by Joseph Wood Krutch; *The Universe and Dr. Einstein,* by Lincoln Barnett, copyright 1950.
The University of New Mexico Press, Albuquerque: *The House at Otowi Bridge,* by Peggy Pond Church, copyright 1962.
Vanguard Press, Inc., New York: *The Inverted Mountains: Canyons of the West,* edited by Roderick Peattie, copyright 1948.
The Viking Press, Inc., New York: *The Challenge of Man's Future,* by Harrison Brown, copyright 1954, 1958.

The Sierra Club, founded in 1892 by John Muir, has devoted itself to the study and protection of national scenic resources, particularly those of mountain regions. All Sierra Club publications are part of the nonprofit effort the club carries on as a public trust. The club is affiliated with the International Union for Conservation, the Natural Resources Council of America, and the Federation of Western Outdoor Clubs. There are chapters in California, the Pacific Northwest, the Great Basin, the Great Lakes region, and on the Atlantic seaboard. Participation is invited in the program to enjoy and preserve wilderness, wildlife, forests, and streams. *Address: Mills Tower, San Francisco; 25 West 45th Street, New York; 710 Dupont Circle Building, Washington, D. C.*

FOREWORD

Glen Canyon died in 1963 and I was partly responsible for its needless death. So were you. Neither you nor I, nor anyone else, knew it well enough to insist that at all costs it should endure. When we began to find out it was too late. On January 21, 1963, the last day on which the execution of one of the planet's greatest scenic antiquities could yet have been stayed, the man who theoretically had the power to save this place did not find a way to pick up a telephone and give the necessary order. I was within a few feet of his desk in Washington that day and witnessed how the forces long at work finally had their way. So a steel gate dropped, choking off the flow in the canyon's carotid artery, and from that moment the canyon's life force ebbed quickly. A huge reservoir, absolutely not needed in this century, almost certainly not needed in the next, and conceivably never to be needed at all, began to fill. At this writing the rising waters are destined to blot out everything of beauty which this book records.

It is Eliot Porter's gift to be able to reveal this beauty as no other photographer has done. Color is indeed his music, as all will believe who in due course follow him and have any wish to listen to light. I was fortunate enough to do this myself on three trips to Glen Canyon. I learned that you can no more impose preconceptions of color on this place than you can impose patterns of Alpine structure on Colorado River canyon forms. The inner world of the side canyons, walled in shadows, will never know the sun but may catch reflected hues from a high opposite wall. The thin crescent of blue is the inner world's only fragment of sky, and any shiny place in the depths will mirror but distort it. The reflected light cannot be conventional when the incident light is not, but thinking can almost make it so. The camera, however, must come closer to the truth, especially when it is in the hands of a colorist. Eliot Porter's name will be inseparable from the spirit of Glen Canyon, just as John Wesley Powell's is from the discovery of the canyon, because of what his perceptive camera has recorded there.

The best of the canyon is going or gone. Some second-best beauty remains along the Colorado of course, but much of its meaning vanished when Glen Canyon died. The rest will go the way Glen Canyon did unless enough people begin to feel uneasy about the current interpretation of what progress consists of—unless they are willing to ask if progress has really served good purpose if it wipes out so many of the things that make life worthwhile.

Evolution demonstrates the value of learning from mistakes; so perhaps we can evolve a subservient technology—one that follows man instead of leading him. The closing of Glen Canyon dam in our time was a major mistake to learn from, and our purpose here is to help the world remember these things lost.

There could be long and acrimonious debate over the accusation of mistake. Good men, who have plans for the Colorado River whereby "a natural menace becomes a natural resource," would argue tirelessly that the Colorado must be controlled, that its energy should be tapped and sold to finance agricultural development in the arid west. But our point here is that for all their good intentions these men had too insular a notion of what man's relation to his environment should be, and it is tragic that their insularity was heeded. The natural Colorado—what is left of it—is a miracle, not a menace. The menace is more likely the notion that growth and progress are the same, and that the gross national product is the measure of the good life.

It is a well-documented fact that the Colorado River is being overdeveloped. A bookkeeping transaction could have served the ostensible purpose of Glen Canyon dam, which without that transaction emerges as a costly device to make sure water will flow downhill. What water this reservoir holds back for credit above the arbitrary division point of Lee's Ferry could be credited in Lake Mead much more economically and far less wastefully. The dam irrigates nothing. Instead, it evaporates an enormous quantity of water that could otherwise have irrigated land or supplied cities in an arid region that is short of water. To the extent reservoir storage adds to the already high mineral content of the water, the water's quality is diminished for all downstream use, including Mexico's. The transcendent purpose of the dam is to produce hydroelectric power, and the revenues incident thereto, which could finance irrigation of new and costly agriculture—as if there were no way to finance development of a region other than to sacrifice irretrievably its most important scenic assets—assets equaled nowhere else on earth.

Hoover, Parker, and Davis dams already exist and control the river adequately; they could probably continue to do so until Lake Mead is silted in completely, perhaps two hundred years from now. The Colorado-Big Thompson diversion project and developments like it which are already under way or planned will exploit the Colorado's waters upstream, where nearly half the flow has been allocated. Glen Canyon dam is a monument to man's lack of flexibility—to his having concluded that the only way to finance Reclamation is to sell the hydroelectric power produced by falling water of the streams he proposes to irrigate with. Revenue by other routes, including that from other sources of power which are already or will soon be less expensive to develop, was not politically attainable at the moment. This public failure—the inability to finance reasonable development of the West by means that financed it elsewhere—has cost all men, for all time, the miracle of an unspoiled Glen Canyon.

Other miracles will vanish by the same route unless we can learn from this mistake. The plans are well under way to eradicate the finest of those miracles left on the Colorado, as well as on other major rivers. A similar mistake was made early in the century at Hetch Hetchy in the Sierra Nevada, where a second Yosemite, now much needed for its natural beauty, was flooded to provide power for San Francisco. Alternative sources of water and power that could have saved Hetch Hetchy are still unused. Out of that mistake grew the National Park Act of 1916. If the destruction of Glen Canyon leads indirectly to a diminishing of such forces of rapacity or can somehow correct the belief that man's only road to salvation is a paved one, then there will be some amelioration.

The alternatives that could have saved Glen Canyon are still unused. Fossil fuels, for one. The states of the Upper Basin of the Colorado contain a major part of the earth's coal reserves. The development of these resources is in the doldrums—and they are a much longer-lived source of energy than the short-lived reservoirs planned for the silty Colorado. Atomic and solar sources of energy will beyond doubt, generations before Lake Mead is silted in, make the destruction of Glen Canyon appear to have been the most naïve of choices in the search for electricity. Nothing our technology will have taught us, in this century or any other, will be able to put Glen Canyon back together again.

The Place No One Knew has a moral—which is why the Sierra Club publishes it—and the moral is simple: Progress need not deny to the people their inalienable right to be informed and to choose. In Glen Canyon the people never knew what the choices were. Next time, in other stretches of the Colorado, on other rivers that are still free, and wherever there is wildness that can be part of our civilization instead of victim to it, the people need to know before a bureau's elite decide to wipe out what no men can replace. The Sierra Club has no better purpose than to try to let people know in time. In Glen Canyon we failed. There could hardly be a costlier peacetime mistake. With support from people who care, we hope in the years to come to help deter similar ravages of blind progress.

ACKNOWLEDGMENTS

On behalf of the Sierra Club—its members, its publications committee, and its directors— I should like first of all to acknowledge our gratitude to Eliot Porter for finding us, first with the series of photographs and selections from Thoreau which led to "In Wildness . . ." and for his subsequently sending selections from his Glen Canyon Series, 1961 and 1962, which made clear immediately that The Place No One Knew must come into being.

Of hardly less importance is our debt to the people who said what they did so well that it was inevitable that their words should find a way to the text pages facing Eliot Porter's photographs. We recognize that there would have been a pleasant and useful homogeneity had we relied upon one person alone to tell the Glen Canyon story. But when Wallace Stegner (who could have told the story) reviewed the photomanuscript in its strange mixture of wonderful dye-transfer prints and chaotic cut-and-paste text spread around our headquarters, he said that the book is right the way it is: one person's words would have been a voice in the wilderness; we have a chorus instead—many voices, not to be dismissed, for the wilderness. We are grateful for all these voices.

Given one hundred fifty dye-transfer prints of Glen Canyon, we found that the book could evolve swiftly, once we had survived the trauma of eliminating half the prints. The beauty of each photograph is self-sufficient. The beauty is augmented in much of the text, but in parts the textual concepts are not always pleasant; photographs less excellent than Porter's might not have borne the burden the text places upon them. Porter's not only hold up, we feel, but reinforce as well. Their very sculpture adds extra emphasis where none was supplied. What has happened to the sculpture since he photographed it adds poignancy, and it is the presumption of this that imposes continuity on what might sometimes appear to be a tangled skein.

Thanks to the perusing of some sixty books, most of it done by Russell Butcher, we were as hard-pressed in leaving out excerpts of text as we were with casting aside photographs. There is still a very beautiful book in what we are not publishing! Our greatest difficulty was in finding enough about the place—and this difficulty led to our choice of title.

It is one thing to know that you have a book, and another to know how to finance its publication when you are a nonprofit organization and the work to be done exceeds the funds available to do it. We asked several of the people who have been especially interested in Sierra Club books for help, suggesting that the help might be of various kinds—an outright gift which could continue to revolve in the club's publishing program, spreading the conservation story; an interest-free loan contingent upon sales; or an advance order for a quantity of books. We are grateful to the following, who generously responded in one of these ways:
Mrs. Therese P. Atwater, Lavina Betty Bierer, Professor and Mrs. Harold C. Bradley, William C. Bradley, Mr. and Mrs. Wesley Bunnelle, B. C. Cochrane, Norman L. Cram, Randal Dickey, Jr., Dyson Duncan, Walter Meayers Edwards, Charles Eggert, James Harvey Fahs, Fred D.

Fletcher, D. Hanson Grubb, Robert Henigson, Homer D. Kesten, Mrs. James R. Lewis, Norman B. Livermore, Jr., David H. McAlpin, Mr. and Mrs. John W. McKean, Jr., Thomas H. May, Byron S. Miller, Bernard Peyton, Edward C. Porter, John H. Redfern, E. Evelyn Ringemann, Betty Jane Robinson, Bernard J. Sabaroff, Dwight Strong, John Tellaisha, Mrs. Frank Thorp, John B. Thune, David H. Utley, Martha von Briesen, Charles Vogl, Mr. and Mrs. John U. White, and Leela C. Zion.

Still earlier generosity permitted the club to establish the revolving publication fund itself, without which this book—and earlier books—would not have been possible; we are therefore recurringly grateful to the Belvedere Scientific Fund, the McGraw Foundation, the late Inez Mexía, the late Marion Randall Parsons, and to Walter A. Starr—all principal sources of the publications fund.

The most reassuring part of the whole effort to publish the book was the wealth of material we found about the wilderness idea—the *national park* idea, if we go back to the concept that underlay the first great parks and that has been a unique American contribution toward harmony between man and the natural world. We hope that the testimony of the text, combined with Eliot Porter's keen powers of observation, will serve lasting purpose by in some way stepping up the pace with which mankind preserves what is left of the world's irreplaceables.

DAVID BROWER

Berkeley, California
March 13, 1963

CONTENTS

SEVENTY-TWO PLATES

To my children

But where will the chance to know wildness be a generation from now?
How much of the magic of this, the American earth, will have been dozed
and paved into oblivion by the great feats of engineering that seem to come so much
more readily to hand than the knack of saving something for what it is? . . .

Again and again the challenge to explore has been met, handled, and
relished by one generation—and precluded to any other.

THE LIVING CANYON

The architect, the life-giver, and the moderator of Glen Canyon is the Colorado River. It slips along serenely, riffled only in the few places where boulder-filled narrows confine it, for nearly two hundred miles. For all the serenity, the first canyon experience is too overwhelming to let you take in more than the broadest features and boldest strokes. The eye is numbed by vastness and magnificence, and passes over the fine details, ignoring them in a defense against surfeit. The big features, the massive walls and towers, the shimmering vistas, the enveloping light, are all hypnotizing, shutting out awareness of the particular.

Later you begin to focus on the smaller, more familiar, more comprehensible objects which, when finally seen in the context of the whole, are endowed with a wonder no less than the total. It is from them that the greatest rewards come. Then you see for the first time the velvety lawns of young tamarisks sprouting on the wet sandbars just vacated by the retreating flood, or notice how the swirling surface of the green, opaque river converts light reflected from rocks and trees and sky into a moire of interlacing lines and coils of color, or observe the festooned, evocative designs etched into the walls by water and lichens.

It is an intimate canyon. The feeling of intimacy comes partly from your being able to travel through it by boat—from a close association unknown in a canyon seen only from above or dipped into at only a few places. The intimacy also comes from the calmness and congeniality of the river and the closeness of the walls. Life along the banks and bars is unhurried. Every bend offers a good campsite. Clear springs are not far apart, providing in a shaded setting of mossy, dripping rocks and wildflowers welcome respite from the heat of noon. At evening, in the glow of burnished cliffs, a quiet peace settles on the boatmen gathered close to their campfire, their subdued voices accentuating the faint gurgling of the big river slipping past its banks. With night spreading fast and stars appearing in the diminished sky, the canyon's dimly silhouetted walls give comfort and security.

The rocks through which the canyon was carved are old monolithic sandstones rising hundreds of feet, in places straight from the water. The Wingate formation at the upper end weathers through vertical cracks extending down from the surface into massive, burnt-red, columnar blocks and slabs. When these break off and fall, shattering on the steep, narrow talus bordering the river, they strew the slope with upended, jagged fragments; their faces, like the cliff above, oxidize to a polished purple-black. This dark varnish, reflecting the sky, turns in the shade to deep metallic blue but in the sun shines a dazzling white. Downstream the Wingate formation drops out of sight below the surface. Its place is taken by Navajo sandstone, and the character of the cliffs changes strikingly. Here the plateau weathers into round domes and the rim is less sharp. Water streaks the walls with ribbons of color that cling like folds of wet curtains to the rock. The dark stains are caused by the algae and lichens that manage to grow in the occasional films of moisture; the bluish-white bands mark where chemicals have been leached.

The Navajo sandstone cleaves to produce immense arches and bays and all manner of rippled and shell-like structures. Imposed on these shapes, giving emphasis by contrast, oxidation has added to the yellow and orange stone a blue and purple cast; and lichens following the same pattern superimpose on north-facing walls a texture of tapestry. Slabs spall off the cliffs from time to time, one layer after another. The fresh scars and those of great antiquity add their own infinite variety to that of the tapestries. High on the face of the canyon walls in many places, like the pupilless eyes of marble statues, huge lenticular depressions have flaked out—the beginnings of caves, in which water oozes out along the fracture lines. If the caves are shaded, they contain a heavy growth of maidenhair fern and mimulus.

The tributaries of Glen Canyon are a unique natural museum exhibiting examples of erosion found nowhere else in the world. The walls of the canyon as a whole are like worm-eaten wood, riddled with tunnels on an enormous scale. The smooth bores of their unroofed, twisting holes converge on the common river channel. Most of them are quite short, no more than a mile in length, the shortest snaking back only two or three turns before ending abruptly in a circular chamber surrounding a pool into which a trickle may descend through a sculptured channel.

The similarity of the tributary ground plans shows that the same forces were at work molding them. Their courses are S-curves twisting back into the sandstone of the Colorado Plateau. Some straighten out as they advance headward, but others twist for miles back from the river— like Twilight Canyon, which my youngest son followed for fifty-seven turns without coming to an end or detecting a lessening of the height of its walls. It and several other canyons are dry and dead; nothing grows among heaped-up boulders. No flowers spring from the barren walls, and no water stays, unless it is deeply shaded under a massively undercut wall. Such a canyon is no place to be caught in a flash flood.

But most side canyons, even those carrying no permanent stream, are rich with plant life. For all the havoc the floods work against lifeless structures, they are ineffective against the frailest living things which, like the sea algae of a surf-bound coast, bend to their irresistible force and spring back after the torrent has passed, and the power of fertility soon reseeds the plants that are uprooted. Grasses, flowers, canes, and vines cover the sand banks at the bends. Oaks grow almost impenetrably in the sunniest spots and redbud fills the shady corners. Cotton-woods remember where the water was.

Down all the tributaries pour intermittent floods burdened with sand, each grain a chisel able to liberate imprisoned grains from the ancient walls. The streams batter the canyonsides, tearing away all loose material, and gouging out deep troughs. The narrowness of some canyons —their sides may be hundreds of feet high and less than six feet apart at the bottom—is dramatic evidence of the rapidity of erosion. A few evidently started as tight meanders in the surface rock, in which fast corrasion deepened the channels into wide passages beneath interlocking walls. At the sharpest bends the pounding waters have scooped out deep caves, the girdling walls of which envelop an opposite rounded peninsula of rock. These gigantic structures are like loosely articulated elements of an immobile ball and socket joint. If you stand facing outward in the stream bed in one of these caves and look up at the top of the dome-shaped inner wall, you see the sky as a cresent of blue, bounded above by the overhanging dark surface of the cave rising behind you. The magnitude of these awesome shapes expanding over your head out of the confines of the canyon floor is a test of credulity.

Of all the phenomena of the side canyons, it is the light, even in the farthest depths of the narrowest canyon, that evokes the ultimate in awe. In somber, rocky caverns of purple and ocher stone into which the sun rarely strikes, shallow pools glitter brassily from sunlit cliffs high over-head. Wherever there is a damp cleft, maidenhair fern and scarlet lobelia and white columbine grow. Their drooping leaves turn a dusky cyan-green in the blue shadows, creating a subdued, almost funereal atmosphere.

It is reflection that imparts magic to the waters of the Glen Canyon and its tributaries. Every pool and rill, every sheet of flowing water, every wet rock and seep—these mirror with enameled luster the world about. In narrow chasms streams of melted gems flow over purple sand past banks of verdant willow. Small puddles, like shining eyes, fuse the colors of pink rocks and cerulean sky, and wet ripples of mud may do the same thing. In the changing light nothing remains the same from year to year or hour to hour. Flood and drouth, heat and cold, life and death alter the finer details incessantly, but they leave unchanged the grand plan and the enchanting quality of the Colorado's masterwork.

The first explorers of Glen Canyon, the Powell party, well appreciated its beauty and remarked on it often enough in their accounts to have established its reputation as a wonderland of the Colorado. Later visitors probably did not especially notice its finer aspects for they were lured there by the hope of sudden riches. They came in barges with tools and dredges and machinery to extract gold from the river's sands and gravel benches, but they were frustrated by the difficulties of their operations and returned with empty hands, losing even the wealth they had invested. They left a more permanent mark than their scratchings or the disintegrating machinery they abandoned—the names they gave to the places where they strived, lost heart, and died. Their memorials are places like Smith Bar, California Bar, Klondike and Dead Man bars, and Stanton's Dredge—crazily tilted and rusting in mid river.

But now another kind of invasion is taking place—one that will obliterate all the places that bear the nostalgic names, wipe them out for all foreseeable time. Thus, with nothing tangible to evoke the past, even the memory of the river's history will be destroyed. This final act of destruction is, as it was with Colorado River goldseekers fifty years ago, materially motivated. The wealth of the Colorado this time is its power, ostensibly at least, although there are those who see a less forthright purpose—the ambition of a federal bureau to build an empire out of river development, with sincere regard, no doubt, for one kind of public welfare, but with disregard of many less tangible aspects of human well-being. Glen Canyon dam may appear to exemplify this ambition. But neither does its imposing magnitude alone justify it, nor can the dam serve all the beneficial functions attributed to it in the process of obtaining legislative support or as a subsequent apology.

The waters impounded by this plug of artificial stone spread back through Glen Canyon and for one hundred eighty-six miles in all, inundating the sparkling river, swallowing its luminous cliffs and tapestried walls, and extinguishing far into the long, dim, distant future everything that gave it life. As the waters creep into the side canyons, enveloping one by one their mirroring pools, drowning their bright flowers, backing up their clear, sweet springs with stale flood water, a fine opaque silt settles over all, covering rocks and trees alike with a gray slimy ooze. Darkness pervades the canyons. Death and the thickening, umbrageous gloom take over where life and shimmering light were the glory of the river.

Glen Canyon's forms of life have been separated from the world by the canyon's depth as well as by its desert borders. Its vegetation has been reproducing for centuries, most of the species probably arriving from the outside world by way of the river. Its animals, too, are isolated, a few having developed their own races in the flow of evolutionary processes within the restricted canyon environment. The birds are the most conspicuous. It is their nature to live conspicuous lives—they fly. They advertise their presence by song, even when they seem to be skulking in the thickets. In the spring the willow and tamarisk jungles of the river's edge ring with the cheerful sibilance of yellow warblers. From among the broken rocks of dry talus comes the bright chant of the rock wren, and higher up from the cliff side, the canyon wren's deliberate down-scale notes echo melodiously. Added to these sweet songs, there are some unmelodious, comic sounds issuing frequently from the thickets—the harsh clucking, cawing, and whistling of the yellow-breasted chat that lurks mostly unseen in the densest underbrush but occasionally bursts from the top of a bush in awkward, wing-clapping, nuptial flight.

Great blue herons, with their four-toe prints, mark the muddy border of every lagoon and shallow backwash, where they have stood motionless watching for small fish or frogs. Approached too closely, they rise smoothly, legs dangling, their powerful wings beating slowly in unhurried flight down the river.

In the side canyons, along the narrow water courses where deep pools are carved in rock and the flow is clear and constant, lives a small, plump, gray bird with stumpy tail, the water ouzel. A favorite haunt is the narrows in Bridge Canyon, on the trail to Rainbow Bridge. He is truly aquatic, and although not web-footed, he is as much at home in the water as a duck. He makes his living in the flowing streams and cascades of high country and canyons of the west; he cannot live without them and he never departs far from them. He builds his roofed nest and rears his young in the spray of waterfalls. When first encountered he will probably be bobbing on a stone in midstream, and to your astonishment he may suddenly plunge into the foaming water. Over his somber dark gray suit he instantly slips a resplendent jacket of shiny silver bubbles and walks about on the bottom picking up aquatic larvae here and there showing as little concern as he would on dry land. In a moment he pops out again, leaving his bright diving suit behind and, as dry as before he dove in, continues about his business. He is apparently pleased with his mode of life, bursting into song most unexpectedly after emerging from one of his underwater foraging expeditions. He sings his ebullient, varied song throughout the year for no other assignable reason than the sheer joy of doing so, for he is the only audience when he sings unheard in the mist of a thundering cascade.

To the murmuring and chattering by the river, the raven's harsh caw is added now and then from a high ledge or from a point in the air where he has found a balance between the law of gravity and the law of convection. He hangs there, rocking slightly as he drifts and soars, seeking out the current, his black profile punctuating his words. He is a bird of parts, but he is no show-off nor does he hide his talents. He saves a particular quality in his voice for special occasions, and though he cannot sing, he is able to introduce a bell-like quality into his croak which adds a musical touch without melody. He does not live just to exist, but appears to delight in his greatest accomplishment—flight. A small group may spend hours playing in the air currents, soaring effortlessly, chasing one another in an endless game—diving, swooping wing to wing, turning upside down in a wild exuberant melée, racing past the face of a cliff, feeling desperately for the upsurge that will give an advantage, uttering guttural cries that release all their pent-up excitement just as children cry out in their play. Who can say this is not an expression of joy?

But it is dark now, quiet above the bank except for the river's soft voice. I turn in my sleeping bag toward the east, where a faint light is just perceptible. Soon it will give way to the waxing twilight of morning and the world will fill with color. This is a positive time, a time of expansion and increase and expectation. In the waning twilight of evening everything is closing down and in retreat, but at dawn each moment is brighter; the path into light, into activity, is full of hope and renewed energy and the promise of clarity. The sun, still a long way beneath the rim, routs the last stars down the brightening sky. They make a pale stand in the thinning shadow of the earth, until Venus alone holds out, resisting the stampede. Directly overhead fleecy clouds sail from the northwest across the narrow, rock-enclosed sky, preserving the order of their ranks while their shapes shift and flow. A tinge of pink is spreading over them, changing gradually to salmon and then to yellow, when suddenly from some notch in the horizon the sun bursts into this hemisphere. It lights the top of a butte, transforming it into a metallic crown. Slowly the color slips down its sides, copperplating them and enveloping the canyon in warmth. The river, still in shadow, picks up color and multiplies it, converting gray stones along its muddy bank into uncut lapis lazuli embedded in molten bronze. Blue highlights thread the dry sand ripples. Day is near and will soon blaze into the canyon depths.

All the bizarre morning colors fade with the day's advance. Purple banks and blue dunes become common mud and sand. The river becomes muddy green. The rocks turn to brick and clay as the sun climbs above the canyon rim.

We have our breakfast, pack our few possessions, and are ready to shove off into the current lapping at the loaded boats. We check the sands again for forgotten objects, postponing the final moment, loath to depart the little world which for a night's stop was the focus of our lives in an eternity of timeless existence. We push the boats out, wading knee deep in mud to gain the deeper water before climbing on board. The day is bright and still. No wind ruffles the glassy surface of the river, lined with swirling striae by the upwelling current. The mirrored sandstone cliffs are distorted near the boat, but down the river's reach they are nearly perfectly reflected. In the winding canyon dark and light reflections replace one another in slow succession. The gentle wake of the boat breaks these images into undulating spots and patches, each wave for a moment holding a fragment of sky mixed with golden globules of sunlit rock.

The striped walls of Glen Canyon pass slowly by, progressively revealing and concealing the breaks in their defenses. Often the walls are so sharply undercut by the river that there is no talus, not even a sand bank or bar, to separate them from the water. Some of them are sliced unexpectedly by narrow perpendicular slots. At high water the river deposits its load in them—sand dropping in the eddies at the entrances and finer sediments precipitating in the quietest waters. Back in the slots these fingers of the river blend into a bank of gray ooze which thickens into a slippery bed of clay of uncertain depth extending from wall to wall. After the spring run-off has subsided and the river withdrawn, these slots are left plugged to their mouths with mud and silt that dries slowly to a cracked, crusted surface you can walk on. But the first local freshet will wash it all out.

Like the half-concealed passages into long forgotten tombs, these narrow slots give no hint of the strange sights inside their portals. We plunge apprehensively into the mud and water. Sometimes it is waist-deep; sometimes we have to swim. We struggle through the sucking clay, one laborious step at a time, to harder ground where we make our unimpeded way within.

In Anasazi Canyon, after traversing a winding corridor of tangled woodbine gardens, we find ourselves at last in a circular arena, confronted by overhanging, inaccessible walls. Dark viridescent lumps of moss dot the surface and, trembling in a perpetual current of air, green fern tenacles grow around them from the slippery rock. From a groove at a higher level a thin stream slides into a black and fathomless pond. The whole interior of this tenebrous chamber, with wavy greenery lining its sides, is like the ciliated cavity of a huge sea anemone.

In Cathedral Canyon, beyond a series of immense, vaulted bends, we come to a sudden closing in of the walls where the floor disappears into a water-filled trough no wider than a man's body. Swimming through it is a dreamlike adventure. Shivering, we glide along like seals, chin deep in the water, through still depths into an inscrutable solitude. Only the hollow sound of our splashing reverberates along the contorted channel back into the stony labyrinth. Now and then the mysterious bottom, a stone or a graveled ledge, rises to surprise us. We climb over wedged boulders from one ribbon pool to another in a journey reminiscent of Xanadu, "through caverns measureless to man." A sudden shaft of sun, giving a dimension of reality, penetrates the upper stories through an unseen window. It lights a strip of wall a dazzling yellow and is reflected to our eyes at water level from the thin curved edge where the pool laps the rock in gentle undulations, like golden threads reaching ahead to delineate for a moment the wavering separation of water from stone. At the end a wisp of a waterfall drops from unseen heights overhead, slipping over a smooth and algaed chute into a slatey pool. Shivering, we retrace our way, glad to emerge at last into the August sun.

Little Arch, we discover, is a short canyon, ending in a waterfall up which an earlier explorer cut shallow steps in the wet sandstone. We follow these and are led through pools in a tortured narrow trough to a roofed room in the ocherous rock. It is dry on one side where a sand bank is heaped up; the other side extends a few feet into a moist alcove giving egress—through a chimney leading straight up to the sky—to the free air of the plateau high overhead. The sides of the chimney have been ground into concave plaques lying one above the other like immense elongated scales. An infernal light spreads down this tube and suffuses the chamber, dyeing our faces and half-naked bodies a dull furnace red. Our imaginations, turning to the violent events that must periodically take place in this cavern, picture the enveloping spray and hear the roar of water as it pours down the chimney in a tumultuous, thundering rush.

Weather in the canyon country is not always good. Storms sweep over it from the northwest, the outriggers of disturbances down from the Aleutians, and may last for a week, enveloping the canyon in mist and rain. More usually, summer's bad weather is local and short-lived. Storms develop over the bordering plateaus, spreading out over the encircling land until darkening thunderheads rumble their warning. Down in the canyon, where the cliff-edged sky is narrow, they can surprise you. A white-edged, black cloud rises above the canyon rim, lightning flickers, a crash ricochets down the canyon, and the first drops spatter dark wet circles on the red sandstone. They evaporate quickly from the hot surface but their replacements come fast. A dusty smell pervades the hot air. The rain curves into the canyon in gusts, bright points and streaks against dark cliffs. The drops seem to float down but they strike the face hard. The black cloud now possesses the entire opening of sky and a cold wind sweeps through the canyon. Another flash of lightning brightens the obscurity and thunder crashes again, much louder, reverberating from higher terraces, rolling and rumbling up and down the gorge, dying in the cul de sacs. The rain comes down hard now. The wet cliffs have lost all color, but glisten like mercury from the sheets of water pouring over them. Through the notches and dips in the rim, wherever the walls were streaked, streams pour down. Through larger notches torrents spume over, freefalling hundreds of feet with a roar, some white and clean, others brown and murky. The noise of falling water and the rush of the rising creek drown out all but the thunder.

The downpour retreats as quickly as it came, and the waterfalls diminish, then cease. The sun comes out again, the rocks dry off, a few puddles lingering in their hollows, and the trees glitter and drip briefly. The creek runs brown and full and is the last to return to its peaceful pace.

In the canyon itself the days flow through your consciousness as the river flows along its course, without a break and with hardly a ripple to disturb their smoothness. Problems fade from the forefront of your mind. Duration becomes a serene timeless flow without landmarks, without interruptions, without the insistent beckoning of obligations. The river supplies and in a sense supplants the need for a measure of time. The current becomes the time on which you move. Things happen and days pass. They exist simply in a heap of impressions and memories, all different and yet all of one kind. There is no more liberating or healing experience. It penetrates to the very core of being, scattering anxieties, untangling knots, re-creating the spirit.

To put the world, and yourself at the same time, in a valid perspective you must remove yourself from the demands of both. The world's demands fade the faster, but nonetheless surely your own will shrink to acceptable proportions and cannot sally forth to attack you. In the wilderness of Glen Canyon you do not assail yourself. You glide on into the day unpursued, living, as all good river travelers should, in the present.

ELIOT PORTER

THE PLACE

Drifting here, you learned to perceive, not to preconceive, what makes a land beautiful. Beauty is where you see it and you saw it often where the big river, thin-edged with green, slid along under the pastel tapestries. An old river had built the stone grain by grain, and the new river was shaping it—imperceptibly aided by artists who left long ago. You didn't quite catch the river in the act of sculpturing, but the color of the Colorado assured you that creation was still going on.

When your spirit cries for peace, come to a world of canyons
deep in an old land; feel the exultation of high plateaus,
the strength of moving waters, the simplicity of sand and grass,
and the silence of growth. — AUGUST FRUGÉ

Perhaps this planet does somewhere else contain a thing like the Colorado River—but that is no matter; we at any rate in our continent possess one of nature's very vastest works. After the River and its tributaries have done with all sight of the upper world, have left behind the bordering plains and streamed through the various gashes which their floods have sliced in the mountains that once stopped their way, then the culminating wonder begins. The River has been flowing through the loneliest part which remains to us of that large space once denominated "The Great American Desert" by the vague maps in our old geographies. — OWEN WISTER

Out of this vast network of rivers emerges the Colorado itself.
Dominating land and man, it is the greatest single fact within an area of
nearly a quarter million square miles. Bigger than its statistics, it is
one of the great rivers of the world . . .

And this at last seems the ultimate task to which the Colorado is
appointed . . . to move bodily, sand by sand and peak by peak, through the
measureless millenniums man calls eternity, the whole great
Colorado Pyramid out into the sea. — FRANK WATERS

Captain Dutton, Powell's particular protege . . . found, as everyone who ever attempted to write about that country has found, that word pictures are about as inadequate as painted ones. The country is too big . . . Add to the enormous size the delicate shadings of color, changing at every hour of the day, with every passing cloud, and the peculiarly architectural, almost symmetrical forms that erosion has filled the canyon with, and the job becomes almost impossible. For all that, Dutton not only tried to describe it, but did. His monographs are at least half nature writing . . .

They were monumental men in a monumental country doing a monumental job. No one knows the plateau and canyon country if he does not know the work of Powell and Dutton and Holmes and Hayden and Gilbert. There has seldom been a group of similar stature gathered together on one project. They added something to that country by their presence there. — WALLACE STEGNER

For endless miles, in all the formations, the forms are as repetitive as if carved to a master plan, the strata level or nearly so, the thickness and colors persistent or changing only by imperceptible degrees.

Dutton first taught the world to look at that country and see it as it was . . . . He was a student of form, as of color, and he dismissed the alpine, craggy forms among which the romantic imagination has loved to wander since Childe Harold showed it how. Those alpine forms, which are "only big and rough," do not appear in the Plateau Province. The forms that do appear have no counterparts among those which have shaped and trained our appreciation. — WALLACE STEGNER

This ornamentation is suggestive rather than precise . . . But though exact symmetry is wanting, nature has here brought home to us the truth that symmetry is only one of an infinite range of devices by which beauty can be materialized.

And finer forms are in the quarry
Than ever Angelo evoked.

— CLARENCE E. DUTTON

The lover of nature, whose perceptions have been trained in the Alps, in Italy, Germany, or New England, in the Appalachians or Cordilleras, in Scotland or Colorado, would enter this strange region with a shock, and dwell there for a time with a sense of oppression, and perhaps with horror. Whatsoever things he had learned to regard as beautiful and noble he would seldom or never see, and whatsoever he might see would appear to him as anything but beautiful and noble. Whatsoever might be bold or striking would at first seem only grotesque. The colors would be the very ones he had learned to shun as tawdry and bizarre. The tones and shades, modest and tender, subdued yet rich, in which his fancy had always taken special delight, would be the ones which are conspicuously absent. But time would bring a gradual change. Some day he would suddenly become conscious that outlines which at first seemed harsh and trivial have grace and meaning; that forms which seemed grotesque are full of dignity; that magnitudes which had added enormity to coarseness have become a replete with strength and even majesty; that colors which had been esteemed unrefined, immodest, and blaring, are as expressive, tender, changeful, and capacious of effects as any others. Great innovations, whether in art or literature, in science or in nature, seldom take the world by storm. They must be understood before they can be estimated, and must be cultivated before they can be understood. — CLARENCE E. DUTTON

. . . Very wonderful at times is the sculpture of these majestic walls. There is an architectural style about it which must be seen to be appreciated. The resemblances to architecture are not fanciful or metaphorical, but are real and vivid; so much so that the unaccustomed tourist often feels a vague skepticism whether these are truly the works of the blind forces of nature or of some intelligence akin to the human but far mightier; and even the experienced explorer is sometimes brought to a sudden halt and filled with amazement by the apparition of forms as definite and eloquent as those of art. Each geological formation exhibits in its cliffs a distinct style of architecture which is not reproduced among the cliffs of other formations, and these several styles differ as much as those which are cultivated by different races of men. — CLARENCE E. DUTTON

10. *Wall detail, talus and twisted ledges*

... In no other portion of the world are the natural laws governing the processes of land sculpture exemplified so grandly; nowhere else are their results set forth so clearly. — CLARENCE E. DUTTON

Glen Canyon, into which they now floated . . . is completely different.
As beautiful as any of the canyons, it is almost absolutely serene,
an interlude for a pastoral flute. Except for some riffles in the upper
section its river is wide, smooth, deep, spinning in dignified whirlpools
and moving no more than seven or eight miles an hour. Its walls are the
monolithic Navajo sandstone, sometimes smooth and vertical, rounding
off to domes at the rims, sometimes undercut by great arched caves,
sometimes fantastically eroded by slit side canyons, alcoves, grottos
green with redbud and maiden-hair and with springs of sweet water.

— WALLACE STEGNER

. . . and in a shadow, look about you and see if there is not plenty of color there, too. The walls are dyed with it, the stones are stained with it—all sorts of colors from strata of rock, from clays and slates, from minerals, from lichens, from mosses. —JOHN C. VAN DYKE

If there is magic on this planet,
it is contained in water. — LOREN EISELEY

Let us not underrate the versatility and resources of Nature, nor question
her good taste, for she has made these walls as full of life, variety, and
expression as any others, and yet has conserved the noble dignity of
which simplicity is an essential part. Instead of a straight, unbroken
palisade, which would be tame indeed, the wall is exceedingly sinuous and
angular, here throwing out a bastion, there deeply recessed by a bay.
Many chasms are cut through it, cleaving from top to bottom. Many
great buttes and isolated temples stand out from the parent mass, and the
masses so isolated often weather into domes and half-domes of bald white
rock which look a calm defiance of human intrusion.

— CLARENCE E. DUTTON

Time, geologic time, looks out at us from the rocks as from no other objects in the landscape. Geologic time! How the striking of the great clock, whose hours are millions of years, reverberates out of the abyss of the past! Mountains fall and the foundations of the earth shift as it beats out the moments of terrestrial history. Rocks have literally come down to us from a foreworld. The youth of the earth is in the soil and in the trees and verdure that spring from it; its age is in the rocks . . . Even if we do not know our geology, there is something in the face of a cliff and in the look of a granite boulder that gives us pause . . .

The rocks have a history; gray and weatherworn, they are veterans of many battles; they have most of them marched in the ranks of vast stone brigades during the ice age; they have been torn from the hills, recruited from the mountaintops, and marshaled on the plains and in the valleys; and now the elemental war is over, there they lie waging a gentle but incessant warfare with time and slowly, oh, so slowly, yielding to its attacks! I say they lie there, but some of them are still in motion, creeping down the slopes or out from the claybanks, nudged and urged along by the frosts and the rains and the sun. — JOHN BURROUGHS

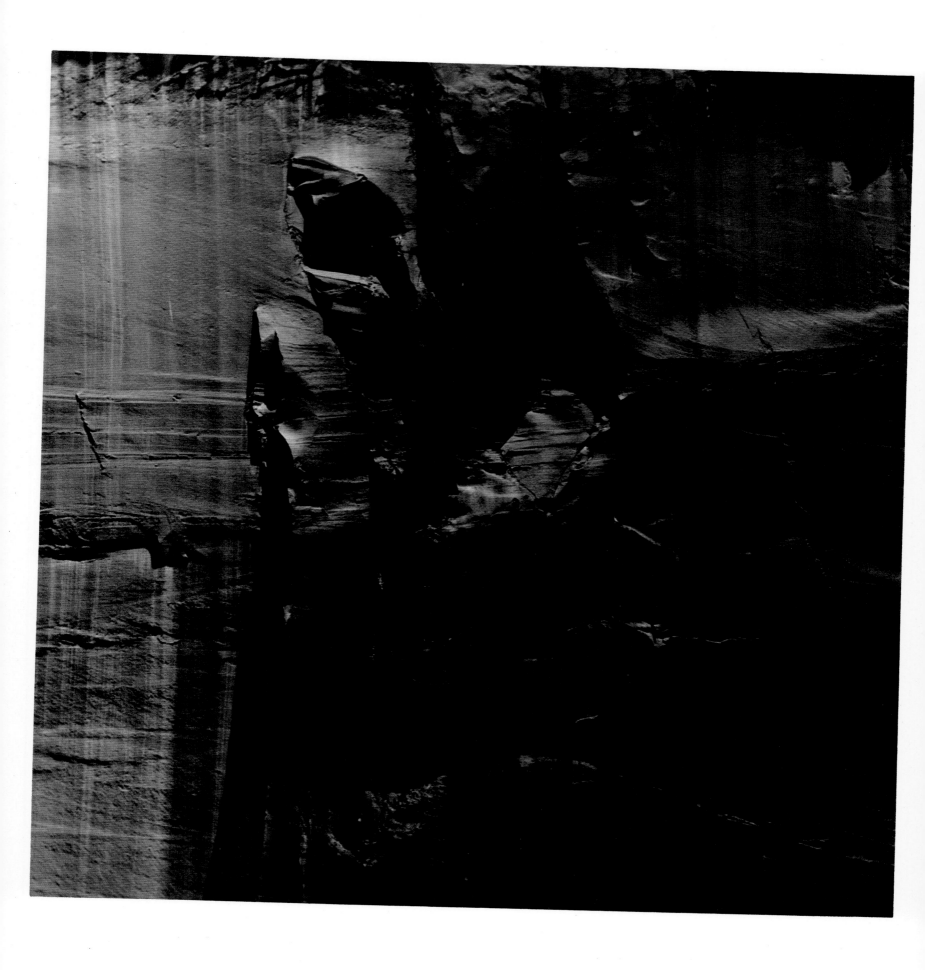

. . . The earth [Hutton] says, like the body of an animal, is wasted at the same time that it is repaired. It has a state of growth and augmentation; it has another state, which is that of diminution and decay. This world is thus destroyed in one part, but it is renewed in another . . .

He saw the bit of soil carried away by a mountain brook or a spring freshet lodge in and nourish a lower valley; he saw the wind endlessly polishing and eroding stones on the high flanks of the world.

— LOREN EISELEY

Here the earth has had a slow, regular pulse. It rose and fell for millions of years under Carboniferous, Permian, Triassic oceans, under Cretaceous seas, under the fresh-water lakes of the Eocene, before it was heaved up and exposed to rain and frost and running water and the sandblast winds. Mountains were carved out of its great tables and domes, river systems cut into it and formed canyons, elevations were weathered and carried away. What had accumulated pebble by pebble and grain by grain, cemented with lime and silica, folding into itself the shells of sea life, scales of fishes, the compacted houses of corals, began to disintegrate again. Vast cyclic changes have left only traces. Though the geological record in the Plateau Province is probably as clear as it is anywhere on earth, the boundary between ignorance and knowledge, between speculation and certainty, is often no more than a line of ancient fracture almost obliterated, or an enigmatic unconformity between two layers of rock, or a slight but significant change from salt water to brackish water fossils. — WALLACE STEGNER

18. *Pool and reflection, Grand Gulch*

Human history in that country is almost as tentative, and to our foreshortening eyes nearly as long. A vague sort of knowledge, with plenty of speculation to accompany it, reaches back to that all-but-Eozoic time when the Ho-ho-kam in the southwestern desert and the Anasazi among the plateaus built their mortared houses and granaries, and lived for certain years whose remoteness is measurable by the fading radioactivity of their dead campfires, and were driven out by certain causes including drouths known to us by the starved growth rings of ancient trees. Gradually, over several generations, we have sorted out a kind of stratigraphy of the plateau peoples: Basket-Maker I, Basket-Maker II, Post-Basket-Maker, Pre-Pueblo, Pueblo I, II, or III. . . . We can mark the unconformities between strata of human history, and knowledge broadens down, not quite from precedent to precedent, but from inference to inference, toward historical time. . . . Though we may be often and for long periods on solid ground, we are never quite out of sight of the half-effaced shorelines of speculation. Knowledge extends in promontories and bays; or to put it vertically rather than horizontally, the strata from remote to recent never lie so unbroken that we cannot find some line of unconformity where the imagination must make a leap. There are so many horizons, geological and human, where the evidence is missing or incomplete. — WALLACE STEGNER

None but Indians have ever lived in this country, and they exist only as a part of it. They have never attempted to assert themselves, but have grown up in it like the trees. It is their food, their drink, their religion, and their life. Their songs and prayers are all of the earth, the sky, and the rain. They never struggle with it, but use it to help them only as a part of themselves. They pass through it silently, leaving as little trace as sunlight through wind.— DONALD JOHN HALL

Man's greatest experience—the one that brings supreme exultation—
is spiritual, not physical. It is the catching of some vision of the universe
and translating it into a poem or work of art, into a Sermon on the
Mount, into a Gettysburg Address, into a mathematical formula that
unlocks the doors of atomic energy. This is a drive that develops early in
life. Boys have it. The lad who picks up an arrowhead in the woods has
established his first vivid and dramatic contact with history. It was the
hand of a redman, now dead for centuries perhaps, that found this stone
of agate or obsidian and fashioned from it a jagged-edged knife point to
drop a rabbit or deer. Having received it from the redman, this boy
walks for a moment by the redman's side in a long, silent,
swinging stride.— WILLIAM O. DOUGLAS

This place exerts a magnetic spell. The sky is there above it but not of it. Its being is apart; its climate, its light, its own. The beams of the sun come into it like visitors. Its own winds blow through it, not those of outside, where we live. The River streams down its mysterious reaches, hurrying ceaselessly; sometimes a smooth sliding lap, sometimes a falling, broken wilderness of billows and whirlpools. Above stand its walls, rising through space upon space of silence. They glow, they gloom, they shine.

— OWEN WISTER

It is lovely and terrible wilderness . . . harshly and beautifully colored, broken and worn until its bones are exposed, its great sky without a smudge or taint from Technocracy, and in hidden corners and pockets under its cliffs the sudden poetry of springs. Save a piece of country like that intact, and it does not matter in the slightest that only a few people every year will go into it. That is precisely its value. . . . But those who haven't the stength or youth to go into it and live with it can still drive up onto the shoulder of the Aquarious Plateau and simply sit and look. They can look two hundred miles, clear into Colorado; and looking down over the cliffs and canyons of the San Rafael Swell and the Robbers' Roost they can also look as deeply into themselves as anywhere I know. And if they can't even get to the places on the Aquarius where the present roads will carry them, they can simply contemplate the idea, take pleasure in the fact that such a timeless and uncontrolled part of earth is still there. — WALLACE STEGNER

Now the whole enormous drainage basin of the river was floating them, melted snow from the high Wind River peaks, and from the Wasatch, and from the Uintas with their hundred cold streams, Black's Fork, Henry's Fork, Ham's Fork, Kingfisher Creek, Brush Creek, the Uinta; the western slopes of the Colorado Rockies whose creeks poured into the Yampa and the White; the waters all the way from Grand Lake under the shadow of Long's Peak, and the tributary springs and creeks and runoff gulches that fed the Grand all the way to modern Grand Junction and Moab; and finally the San Juan, muddy from recent rains, its headwaters tangled with those of the Rio Grande in the Five Rivers country of southwest Colorado, its gathering waters coming down from the San Juan Mountains through New Mexico and what would sometime be Arizona and across the southeastern corner of Utah through the country of the Navajo. It was a big river by now, a tremendous surge . . .

WALLACE STEGNER [*about the Powell party, 1869*]

Powell's Journal describes a side-canyon discovery:
"August 1 — We drop down two miles this morning, and go into camp again. There is a low, willow-covered strip of land along the walls on the east. Across this we walk, to explore an alcove which we see from the river. . . .

"...On entering, we find a little grove of box-elder and cottonwood trees; and, turning to the right, we find ourselves in a vast chamber, carved out of the rock. At the upper end there is a clear, deep pool of water, bordered with verdure. Standing by the side of this, we can see the grove at the entrance. ..."

"...The waters from the bare rocks back of the canyon, gathering rapidly into a small channel, have eroded a deep side canyon, through which they run, until they fall into the farther end of this chamber. The rock at the ceiling is hard, the rock below, very soft and friable; and having cut through the upper harder portion down into the lower and softer, the stream has washed out these friable sandstones; and thus the chamber has been excavated. ...

28. Stream below Music Temple

". . . Here we bring our camp. When 'Old Shady' sings us a song at night, we are pleased to find that this hollow in the rock is filled with sweet sounds. It was doubtless made for an academy of music by its storm-born architect; so we name it Music Temple." — JOHN WESLEY POWELL

Some night lie at the mouth of a rock-carved amphitheater two or three times the size of anything you've ever been in. Look up the two-thousand-foot wall to the billion stars and listen to the murmuring of the river still carving deeper the slot of canyon you're in. Think of nothing but what you see and feel and hear and smell.

What a campsite we had picked! . . . Beyond us, the river made a lazy curve to the left and there the canyon wall rose straight up a thousand feet. For a mile and a half this cliff followed the river before the wall fell back again. The face of the cliff was stained with long, black streamers from the water which cascaded over the rim in wet weather. It was an imposing sight, a gigantic backdrop — a motionless hanging tapestry . . .

— CHARLES EGGERT

Hidden Passage—it was well-named. I could not make it stand forth to be seen. . . . I looked ahead to where both walls drew in upon each other, curving away into what must be yet another mighty coil beyond my sight, and walked slowly on.

On one side above me the red and gold wall was streaked with organ pipes of black and rose and taupe, and on the other, a drift of fringed veil hung delicately purple across its topaz face. Around me now on both walls, within my reach, ran an even band some six feet wide of maidenhair and ribbon fern, moist, brilliantly green and trailing downward as if from a window box. Below it were powder-blue spears where water had left its mark. Both green and blue were reflected in the stream that lay mirror still right here. I walked beside it on a cool border of yellow sand that narrowed more and more as I went on. — CID RICKETTS SUMNER

In the face of immensity it may be that the mind, to preserve its sanity, seeks relief in something small and comprehensible. It was while we were standing there that I was struck by two things insignificant in themselves and worth remembering only because of the effect they had on me. One was a small bird, slight and swift, of the swallow family perhaps. It flew among the pines that stood behind us. Then, with the utmost daring, it went on, on, out over space. Of course I knew that the air was the same there as above solid ground, I knew it was quite unreasonable of me to feel such admiration.

The other thing that struck me was a nosegay of what looked to be ground phlox. It grew just over the edge of the gorge out of no more than a spoonful of soil lodged on solid rock, with not even a small crevice to support it. — CID RICKETTS SUMNER

...in Hidden Passage, where so few had ever come, was a new kind of wonder for me, related less to time than to eternity, akin to something greater than mankind. ...No simple prose was adequate. Poetry, perhaps? I got out my notebook and pencil and tried:

To Hidden Canyon come with reverence.
It is a holy place, this nautilus,
This mighty, spiral-chambered carven shell.
Step softly here where seldom man has trod—
So Adam walked in Eden's virgin dell
That lay still dewy from the hand of God.

But what good were such words as these, telling those who would never come the proper manner of their coming?— CID RICKETTS SUMNER

All things hidden lead us on and on.
The root and end of man are secret things,
But in this rocky heart of solitude
The fearful, deep, primeval silence brings
A kind of answer to our WHITHER? WHENCE?
A whisper that can almost tell us WHY.

— CID RICKETTS SUMNER

. . . what I will always remember about Hidden Passage is the upper
waterfall at the head of the Canyon. There the corridor widens out into a
vaulted hall at the head of which a slender thread of water falls into a
clear pool. From the twilit room we looked up to the overhanging walls
far above us, enclosing a narrow slit of sky between. — WELDON HEALD

We were up early and on the trail before the sun had reached down to us. The rough track followed the little stream in the canyon floor, crossing and recrossing it as we ascended. Along the creek diminutive waterfalls alternated with deep clear pools banked with ferns and overhung with willows and oaks. . . .

A mile up Bridge Canyon we turned a corner. Ahead of us, framed in a V-shaped notch formed by the upper canyon walls, hung a bow of stone against the sky . . .

The real wonder of Rainbow Bridge is that of water carving stone; of the billions of storms which brought the water, of the stone itself, laid down ages ago as drifting sand dunes on a Jurassic desert. The wonder is the sun, the wind, the clouds, vegetation, chemical action, the forces within the earth—all working together for millions of years to produce this perfect masterpiece. — WELDON HEALD

Imagine a structure so massive that the evolutions of the ages have merely brought to the surface its muscular structure, divesting it of weak and useless particles. — CHARLES L. BERNHEIMER

This is a day when life and the world seem to be standing still — only time and the river flowing past the mesas. I cannot work. I go out into the sunshine to sit receptively for what there is in this stillness and calm. I am keenly aware that there is something. Just now it seemed to flow in a rhythm around me and then to enter me — something which comes in a hushed inflowing. All of me is still and yet alert, ready to become part of this wave that laps the shore on which I sit. — EDITH WARNER

There is beauty for the ear in the wilderness.

— WILLIAM O. DOUGLAS

The finest workers in stone are not copper or steel tools,
but the gentle touches of air and
water working at their leisure
with a liberal allowance of time.

— HENRY DAVID THOREAU

Sometimes the rare, the beautiful can only emerge or survive in isolation. In a similar manner, some degree of withdrawal serves to nurture man's creative powers. The artist and scientist bring out of the dark void, like the mysterious universe itself, the unique, the strange, the unexpected. — LOREN EISELEY

By the side of religion, by the side of science, by the side of poetry,
stands Natural Beauty, not as a rival to these,
but as the common inspirer and nourisher of them all.

— G. M. Trevelyan

All Nature is but Art unknown to thee;
All chance direction, which thou canst not see;
All discord, harmony not understood;
All partial evil, universal good:
And spite of Pride, in erring Reason's spite,
One truth is clear, Whatever is, is right.

— Alexander Pope

THE IDEA

We shall seek a renewed stirring of love for the earth; we shall urge that what man is capable of doing to the earth is not always what he ought to do; and we shall plead that all Americans, here, now, determine that a wide, spacious, untrammeled freedom shall remain in the midst of the American earth as living testimony that this generation, our own, had love for the next.

The wilderness and the idea of the wilderness is one of the permanent homes of the human spirit. Here, as many realized, had been miraculously preserved, until the time when civilization could appreciate it, the richness and variety of a natural world which had disappeared unnoticed and little by little from Europe. America was a dream of something long past which had suddenly become a reality. It was what Thoreau called the great "poem" before many of its fairest pages had been ripped out and thrown away. The desire to experience that reality rather than to destroy it drew to our shores some of the best who have ever come to them. — JOSEPH WOOD KRUTCH

We are waking now from the American dream to realize that it was a
dream few Americans lived in their waking hours. The history of the
New World has turned out to be not so different from that of the Old.
The peril that threatens the last of the American wilderness arises
not from the reckless dream, but from the same historic forces of
rapacity and cruelty that laid waste the land in the Mediterranean Basin,
in Arabia, India, and the treeless uplands of China.

The wilderness is there, however, to recall the dream. And lately
we have won a reprieve through the advance of scientific understanding.

The frontier of understanding has no limits, and the curse of want
and poverty may yet be lifted from the life of our species.
That frontier cannot be exploited on the same selfish terms as the
frontier that lies behind. — GERARD PIEL

. . . Have any people on earth ever changed the face of their country as fast
as we Americans? The Egyptians who made up in slave labor what we
possess in bulldozers and power saws had nothing like our speed,
and it took them more than a millennium to arrive at the desert which
is theirs today. . . .

  We do our engulfing in the name of progress; nothing must impede
"the wheels of progress," and nothing does. Today those wheels which
have the light touch of a tank are being accelerated by the pressure of
numbers . . . Like lava from Etna, this pressure overflows the countryside,
filling in meadows and marshes, felling the woodlands, forcing the
brooks underground. Nothing is impregnable. — EDWARD WEEKS

Man is whole when he is in tune with the winds, the stars, and the hills as well as with his neighbors. Being in tune with the apartment or the community is part of the secret. Being in tune with the universe is the entire secret. Man's greatest mission is to preserve life, not to destroy it. When the land becomes the symbol of sterility and poverty, when the wonders of creation have been destroyed, youth has no place to go but the alleys, and a blight lies across the land. — WILLIAM O. DOUGLAS

46. Wall detail, fractured Wingate sandstone

The only possible force that could be motivating the effort to preserve
natural areas is the moral conviction that it is right—that we owe it to
ourselves and to the good earth that supports us to curb our avarice
to the extent of leaving a few spots untouched and unexploited.

   ...I think that when future philosophers scan back through the records
of human history and human thought they may put their finger on this
century as a time of outstanding advance in man's feeling of responsibility
to the earth. Whether man can succeed in preserving an attractive and
livable world is the problem that lies ahead.—A. STARKER LEOPOLD

. . . do we not already sing our love for and obligations to the land of the free and the home of the brave? Yes, but just what and whom do we love? Certainly not the soil, which we are sending helter-skelter downriver. Certainly not the rivers, which we assume have no function except to turn turbines, float barges, and carry off sewage. Certainly not the plants, of which we exterminate whole communities without batting an eye. Certainly not the animals, of which we have already extirpated many of the largest and most beautiful species. A land ethic of course cannot prevent the alteration, management, and use of these 'resources,' but it does affirm their right to continued existence, and, at least in spots, their continued existence in a natural state.

The disquieting thing in the modern picture is the trophy-hunter who never grows up, in whom the capacity for isolation, perception, and husbandry is undeveloped, or perhaps lost. . . .

To enjoy he must possess, invade, appropriate. Hence the wilderness that he cannot personally see has no value to him. Hence the universal assumption that an unused hinterland is rendering no service to society. To those devoid of imagination, a blank place on the map is a useless waste; to others, the most valuable part. (Is my share in Alaska worthless to me because I shall never go there? Do I need a road to show me the arctic prairies, the goose pastures of the Yukon, the Kodiak bear, the sheep meadows behind McKinley?)

It would appear, in short, that the rudimentary grades of outdoor recreation consume their resource-base; the higher grades, at least to a degree, create their own satisfactions with little or no attrition of land or life. . . . Recreational development is a job not of building roads into lovely country, but of building receptivity into the still unlovely human mind. — ALDO LEOPOLD

Some of this attitude is doubtless left over from the pioneer days, when the individual settler had to carve a place for himself barehanded in a sometimes difficult, if not inimical environment. Under these conditions a certain ruthlessness was sometimes unavoidable in self-defense. At all events the pioneer never had to live with the damage he did, as we do now: he could always cancel out his sins, or at least forget them, by moving on to another virgin spot . . .

. . . we shall have to overthrow the myth of the machine and replace it with a new myth of life, a myth based upon a richer understanding of all organic processes, a sharper insight into man's positive "role in changing the face of the earth" — I deliberately use the words of our great geographer, Carl Sauer — and above all a deeply religious faith in man's own capacity to transform and perfect his own self and his own institutions in cooperative relation with all the forces of nature, and above all, with his fellow men. To put all our hope in the improvement of machines is the characteristic inversion and perversion of values of the present age; and that is the reason that our machines threaten us with extinction, since they are now in the hands of deplorably unimproved men. — LEWIS MUMFORD

And as we lengthen and elaborate the chain of technology that intervenes between us and the natural world, we forget that we become steadily more vulnerable to even the slightest failure in that chain.

The time has long since passed when a citizen can function responsibly without a broad understanding of the living landscape of which he is inseparably a part. — PAUL B. SEARS

. . . The need is not really for more brains, the need is now for a gentler, a more tolerant people than those who won for us against the ice, the tiger, and the bear. The hand that hefted the ax, out of some old blind allegiance to the past, fondles the machine gun as lovingly. It is a habit man will have to break to survive, but the roots go very deep.

— LOREN EISELEY

A world from which solitude is extirpated is a very poor ideal . . .
Nor is there much satisfaction in contemplating the world with nothing
left to the spontaneous activity of nature. — JOHN STUART MILL

I would answer that one's first appreciation is a sense that the creation is still going on, that the creative forces are as great and as active to-day as they have ever been, and that to-morrow's morning will be as heroic as any of the world. *Creation is here and now.* So near is man to the creative pageant, so much a part is he of the endless and incredible experiment, that any glimpse he may have will be but the revelation of a moment, a solitary note heard in a symphony thundering through debatable existences of time. Poetry is as necessary to comprehension as science. It is as impossible to live without reverence as it is without joy.

— HENRY BESTON

54. Flood-rippled sand

Whatever attitude to human existence you fashion for yourself, know that it is valid only if it be the shadow of an attitude to Nature. A human life, so often likened to a spectacle upon a stage, is more justly a ritual. The ancient values of dignity, beauty, and poetry which sustain it are of Nature's inspiration; they are born of the mystery and beauty of the world. Do no dishonour to the earth lest you dishonour the spirit of man.

Hold your hands out over the earth as over a flame. To all who love her, who open to her the doors of their veins, she gives of her strength, sustaining them with her own measureless tremor of dark life. Touch the earth, love the earth, honour the earth, her plains, her valleys, her hills, and her seas; rest your spirit in her solitary places. For the gifts of life are the earth's and they are given to all. . . . — HENRY BESTON

You want a place where you can be serene, that will let you contemplate and connect two consecutive thoughts, or that if need be can stir you up as you were made to be stirred up, until you blend with the wind and water and earth you almost forgot you came from. . . .

There must be room enough for time—where the sun can calibrate the day, not the wristwatch, for days or weeks of unordered time, time enough to forget the feel of the pavement and to get the feel of the earth, and of what is natural and right.

. . . I have not been able to shut out wonder occasionally when I have
looked at the world . . .

Slowly, as I sauntered dwarfed among the overhanging pinnacles, as the
great slabs which were the visible remnants of past ages laid their
enormous shadows rhythmically as life and death across my face, the
answer came to me. Man could contain more than himself. Among these
many appearances that flew, or swam in the waters, or wavered
momentarily into being, man alone possessed that unique ability.

— LOREN EISELEY

He has always sought mastery over the materials of his environment . . .
He holds the head of suns within his hands and threatens with it
both the lives and happiness of his unborn descendants.

Man, in the words of one astute biologist, is "caught in a physiological
trap and faced with the problem of escaping from his own ingenuity."

— LOREN EISELEY

. . . In the man-centered universe of the time, one can appreciate the anguish of the Reverend Mr. Kirby discovering the Age of Reptiles: "Who can think that a being of unbounded power, wisdom, and goodness, should create a world merely for the habitation of a race of monsters, without a single, rational being in it to serve and glorify him?" This is the wounded outcry of the human ego as it fails to discover its dominance among the beasts of the past. Even more tragically, it learns that the world, supposedly made for its enjoyment has existed for untold eons entirely indifferent to its coming. The chill vapors of time and space are beginning to filter under the closed door of the human intellect.

— LOREN EISELEY

59. *Wall detail, tilted strata*

It was then that I saw the flight coming on. It was moving like a little close-knit body of black specks that danced and darted and closed again. It was pouring from the north and heading toward me with the undeviating relentlessness of a compass needle. It streamed through the shadows rising out of monstrous gorges. It rushed over towering pinnacles in the red light of the sun, or momentarily sank from sight within their shade. Across that desert of eroding clay and wind-worn stone they came with a faint wild twittering that filled all the air about me as those tiny living bullets hurtled past into the night.

It may not strike you as a marvel. It would not, perhaps, unless you stood in the middle of a dead world at sunset, but that was where I stood. Fifty million years lay under my feet, fifty million years of bellowing monsters moving in a green world now gone so utterly that its very light was travelling on the farther edge of space. The chemicals of all that vanished age lay about me on the ground. Around me still lay the shearing molars of dead titanotheres, the delicate sabers of soft-stepping cats, the hollow sockets that had held the eyes of many a strange, outmoded beast. Those eyes had looked out upon a world as real as ours; dark, savage brains had roamed and roared their challenges into the steaming night.

Now they were still here, or, put it as you will, the chemicals that made them were here about me in the ground. The carbon that had driven them ran blackly in the eroding stone. The stain of iron was in the clays. The iron did not remember the blood it had once moved within, the phosphorus had forgot the savage brain. The little individual moment had ebbed from all those strange combinations of chemicals as it would ebb from our living bodies into the sinks and runnels of oncoming time.

I had lifted up a fistful of that ground. I held it while that wild flight of south-bound warblers hurtled over me into the oncoming dark. There went phosphorus, there went iron, there went carbon, there beat the calcium in those hurrying wings. Alone on a dead planet I watched that incredible miracle speeding past. It ran by some true compass over field and waste land. It cried its individual ecstasies into the air until the gullies rang. It swerved like a single body, it knew itself and, lonely, it bunched close in the racing darkness, its individual entities feeling about them the rising night. And so, crying to each other their identity, they passed away out of my view.

I dropped my fistful of earth. I heard it roll inanimate back into the gully at the base of the hill: iron, carbon, the chemicals of life. Like men from those wild tribes who had haunted these hills before me seeking visions, I made my sign to the great darkness. It was not a mocking sign, and I was not mocked. As I walked into my camp late that night, one man, rousing from his blankets beside the fire, asked sleepily, "What did you see?"

"I think, a miracle," I said softly, but I said it to myself. —LOREN EISELEY

I know that the word "miraculous" is regarded dubiously in scientific circles because of past quarrels with theologians. The word has been defined, however, as an event transcending the known laws of nature. Since, as we have seen, the laws of nature have a way of being altered from one generation of scientists to the next, a little taste for the miraculous in this broad sense will do us no harm. We forget that nature itself is one vast miracle transcending the reality of night and nothingness. We forget that each one of us in his personal life repeats that miracle. — LOREN EISELEY

We rush to and fro like Mad Hatters upon our peculiar errands, all the time imagining our surroundings to be dull and ourselves quite ordinary creatures. Actually, there is nothing in the world to encourage this idea, but such is the mind of man, and this is why he finds it necessary from time to time to send emissaries into the wilderness in the hope of learning of great events, or plans in store for him, that will resuscitate his waning taste for life. . . . One must seek, then, what only the solitary approach can give — a natural revelation. — LOREN EISELEY

The world grows more crowded year by year and at an ever increasing rate.
Men push farther and farther in their search for "resources" to be
exploited, even for more mere space to occupy. Increasingly they tend to
think of the terrestrial globe as *their* earth. They never doubt their right
to deal with it as they think fit — and what they think fit usually involves
the destruction of what nature has thought fit during many
millions of years. — JOSEPH WOOD KRUTCH

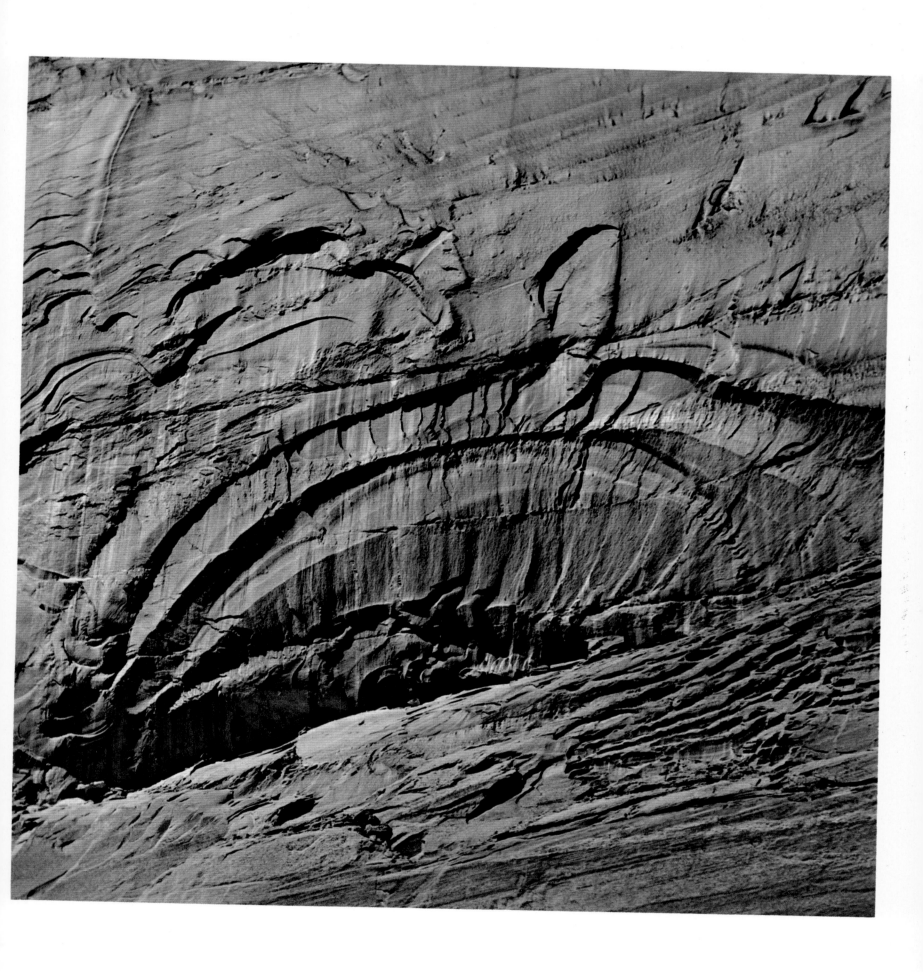

There are always rival claims to every unexploited area, and even the parks cannot stand up against such claims unless the strength of their own claim is recognized. Unless we think of intangible values as no less important than material resources, unless we are willing to say that man's need of and right to what the parks and wildernesses provide are as fundamental as any of his material needs, they are lost. . . .

The generation now living may very well be that which will make the irrevocable decision whether or not America will continue to be for centuries to come the one great nation which had the foresight to preserve an important part of its heritage. If we do not preserve it, then we shall have diminished by just that much the unique privilege of being an American. —JOSEPH WOOD KRUTCH

The world I imagine is one in which people are well fed, well clothed, and well housed. Man, in this world, lives in balance with his environment, nourished by nature in harmony with the myriad other life forms that are beneficial to him. He treats his land wisely, halts erosion and overcropping, and returns all organic waste matter to the soil from which it sprung. He lives efficiently, yet minimizes artificiality. It is not an overcrowded world; people can, if they wish, isolate themselves in the silence of a mountaintop, or they can walk through primeval forests or across wooded plains. In the world of my imagination there is organization, but it is as decentralized as possible, compatible with the requirements for survival. There is a world government, but it exists solely for the purpose of preventing war and stabilizing population, and its powers are irrevocably restricted. The government exists for man rather than man for the government.

In the world of my imagination the various regions are self-sufficient, and the people are free to govern themselves as they choose and to establish their own cultural patterns. All people have a voice in the government, and individuals can move about when and where they please. It is a world where man's creativity is blended with the creativity of nature, and where a moderate degree of organization is blended with a moderate degree of anarchy.

Is such a world impossible of realization? Perhaps it is, but who among us can really say? At least if we try to create such a world there is a chance that we will succeed. But if we let the present trend continue it is all too clear that we will lose forever those qualities of mind and spirit which distinguish the human being from the automaton. — HARRISON BROWN

Something will have gone out of us as a people if we ever let the remaining wilderness be destroyed; if we permit the last virgin forests to be turned into comic books and plastic cigarette cases; if we drive the few remaining members of the wild species into zoos or to extinction; if we pollute the last clear air and dirty the last clean streams and push our paved roads through the last of the silence, so that never again will Americans be free in their own country from the noise, the exhausts, the stinks of human and automotive waste. And so that never again can we have the chance to see ourselves single, separate, vertical and individual in the world, part of the environment of trees and rocks and soil, brother to the other animals, part of the natural world and competent to belong in it. — WALLACE STEGNER

Without any remaining wilderness we are committed wholly, without chance for even momentary reflection and rest, to a headlong drive into our tehnological termite-life, the Brave New World of a completely man-controlled environment. We need wilderness preserved— as much of it as is still left, and as many kinds—because it was the challenge against which our character as a people was formed. The reminder and the reassurance that it is still there is good for our spiritual health even if we never once in ten years set foot in it. It is good for us when we are young, because of the incomparable sanity it can bring briefly, as vacation and rest, into our insane lives. It is important to us when we are old simply because it is there— important, that is, simply as an idea. — WALLACE STEGNER

To live healthily and successfully on the land we must also live with it. We must be part not only of the human community, but of the whole community; we must acknowledge some sort of oneness not only with our neighbors, our countrymen and our civilization but also some respect for the natural as well as for the man-made community. . . .

. . . It is not a sentimental but a grimly literal fact that unless we share this terrestrial globe with creatures other than ourselves, we shall not be able to live on it for long. — JOSEPH WOOD KRUTCH

For all our technological achievements, our very lives tremble upon the delicate scales of nature. We are as ultimately dependent upon the ancient verities of land and sky as were the prehistoric cliff dwellers. Man has not yet completed the full circle toward a realization that his own laws of life must conform in the long view with those greater laws to which he still and forever owes allegiance. . . .

   Man at last has conquered the land. But to what ultimate end no one can say. There is only a vague, inquiet feeling that in all his scheme of domination there is something he might have forgotten. It may well be that the river itself will have the last word, after all. — FRANK WATERS

Those who love the plain, undecorated earth they live on must bow to the urge to reduce stimulating and varied environments to a dead level of human acceptability. This is called progress, and the people who deplore it are in a minority. But the few who know the Colorado will regret its passing as they would mourn the loss of a unique and irreplaceable friend. — WELDON HEALD

Whether you will or not
You are a King, Tristram, for you are one
Of the time-sifted few that leave the world,
When they are gone, not the same place it was.
Mark what you leave.

— EDWIN ARLINGTON ROBINSON

THE GEOLOGY OF GLEN CANYON

Lying between the Sierra Nevada and the Rocky Mountains and encompassing Nevada, Utah, the northern half of Arizona, and parts of Colorado, New Mexico, and California is a great sweep of arid land called the North American Desert. The Great Basin of Nevada and the Colorado Plateau are part of it. Broken by scattered mountain islands but crossed by no great mountain chain except the Uintas in the north, this enormous area takes in the whole upper drainage basin of the Colorado River. The waters that enter its eastern half, whether as rain or as snow on the peaks of its peripheral mountains, flow into the Colorado to be carried to their ultimate destiny—into the air as evaporation from channel, reservoir, and field; by transmountain diversion to distant cities and farms; into the Salton Sea by return flow from irrigation; finally crossing the border into Mexico, where the now almost saline residual waters serve a tenuous agriculture and blend with the ocean salts in the Gulf of California.

The river we know now began many million years ago when on the Colorado Plateau a slow change began that had its origin deep within the crust of the earth. A widespread uplifting of the sedimentary deposits dating back to the Paleozoic Era gradually raised them above the level of the shallow seas which intermittently occupied this region.

During the preceding several hundreds of millions of years, from the first appearance of air-breathing vertebrates until the end of the age of reptiles, hundreds of feet of mud and gravel and sand were deposited, consolidated, and washed away in this area of ever-changing landscape. The material of ancient mountains was spread by streams over low-lying land and carried into the shallow lakes and encroaching oceans. Silt filled in swamps and covered eroded plains until massive layers built up, themselves to be worn away with the rising of the land and the changing of climates. Wet periods were succeeded by dry, and swamps were replaced by deserts when Aeolian ages came into being. Winds swept unimpeded across limitless spaces of rolling dunes for periods which in geological measure were but moments in the kaleidoscopic changes constantly altering the face of the earth. Seas gave way to deserts and deserts, were inundated by advancing seas in a long shifting sequence. Sediments from the dust and debris and rubble of crumbling mountains grew to enormous depths as the earth's crust sank beneath their weight. Deep in the earth or buried under the waters of the seas, these layers were transformed by the cementing action of dissolved lime and iron into the yellow and red sandstones of the Wingate and Navajo formations. Where clay and mud predominated over desert sand, the thinly bedded, shaly Moenkopi and maroon Kayenta strata were deposited, or gray and green uranium-rich beds of Shinarump conglomerate.

At the beginning of the great upwarping the seas drained away and in their place a meandering river carried the waters of the plain into the western ocean. At first, no doubt, it was a sluggish stream, perhaps much like the Mississippi today, flowing through a still rich land and carrying little but the steepings of the soil. Its dark mahogany waters must have supported an abundance of life which in turn supplied the food needs of many of the riparian birds and animals of the Eocene. But as the continent continued to rise, the character of the river changed. Tributaries, loaded with debris, flowing down the western slopes of the newly born Rocky Mountains, gave

165]

it the tools needed to cut its way downward as fast as the land itself was rising. Gouging its way back through time, the river first cut into the last deposits of the late Paleocene laid down more than ten million years earlier; then into the shales and clays formed under the vast swamps of the Cretaceous, backwards for a hundred million years and more; and down through this unimaginable distance in history, scrubbing away particle by particle through the climactic age of the reptiles. The hard sands of the Rocky Mountains were the first tools for this great channelling effort, until the river made its own abrasives from the rocks through which it was flowing, the way diamond dust is used to cut diamonds.

And still restless forces from deep below pushed up the continental crust. Down into ever deeper layers the tireless river, with its burden of grit and powdered rock, ground its way. It dug into the consolidated sediments of the Jurassic, deposited under the shallow seas inhabited by ichthyosaurians and other marine reptilian monsters of that age, and on down into the sands of the Jurassic and Triassic deserts, through the wind-stratified and cross-bedded dunes of the Aeolian period, leaving the age of the dinosaurs far behind, and on through the millions of years of the Permian to the steaming swamps of the Carboniferous—the time of the greatest burgeoning of plant life, when the world's major coal seams were formed and when the first land animals appeared. In places where previous erosion had removed vast thicknesses of Mesozoic or Paleozoic rock, leaving wide unconforming gaps in geological history, the river dug through all the remaining sediments of the Paleozoic to reach and grind into the oldest of all formations on the earth, the hard metamorphic, archaic schists and granites that go back to the time before the appearance of life, a thousand million years in the past. Today still, it is cutting into these rocks, which can be seen exposed on the somber walls of Granite Gorge at the bottom of the Grand Canyon.

To suppose that all these sedimentary layers from the Pre-Cambrian up to the present could be visible anywhere along the river's length is to forget that the processes of building up and tearing down never cease. New rocks are always born from the destruction of the old. Sediments deposited for milleniums out of the debris of older sediments are themselves in turn disintegrated to appear later in still younger deposits, to become consolidated, to be heaved up by tectonic forces, sculptured, and weathered away again. As a consequence of these events, great geological unconformities exist in which one finds sediments in contact with highly eroded underlying formations separated from them by scores of millions of years. Faulting and folding of the crust, interleaved in time with weathering processes, further mixed the strata and produced situations of such complexity that the exact sequence of events is difficult to read.

Forces of erosion were at work on the land above, reducing it too, while the river dug into the past at the bottom of its trench. It was a meandering trench, roughly paralleling the path of the primeval stream, which had here and there been straightened out temporarily by cutting through the narrowing neck of a loop, leaving behind a dry arc of river bed, a rincon, evidence of its once longer course. Much material was blown and washed away, most of it into the river itself through its many tributary canyons. Many of the most recent sediments in the surrounding country have largely disappeared. Their foundations also have been deeply carved, leaving today a ragged land of corniced buttes, of deep canyons, of towering castles whose fretted and sculptured battlements appear to glow with internal fires in the evening light. It is a land, too, of wide valleys and sandy, arid basins and steep-walled, juniper-covered mesas.

The superficial history of this country has probably changed more in recent geological times than the history of the river itself, which was less affected by climatic changes than the plateaus. During the last glacial epoch this country was much more lush than today. Forests of pines clothed the high land where now only a dwarf forest of juniper and pinon grows. Clear streams flowed in all the valleys and canyons which are today watered by occasional, mud-laden flash floods of summer. Grass grew thick and high where now rock-strewn, sandy wastes exist and a sparse desert growth barely holds on.

The part of the upper Colorado River system most difficult of access and least populated lies along either side of the river from Moab south through southern Utah and into northern Arizona as far as the beginning of Grand Canyon. Throughout this whole length the Colorado flows between high canyon walls for a distance of well over three hundred miles. These bordering lands are among the most rugged and impassable in the whole nation. They are cut through and through by innumerable canyons having such precipitous sides that into most of them few trails lead. The surface consists in many places merely of rolling mounds of bare rock, more or less literally petrified sand dunes. Two major tributaries join the Colorado in this desiccated land: the Green River first, upstream on the right, and below it the San Juan from the left, both through formidable canyons. The physiography and historical geology of the canyon divide it naturally into distinct parts named by the early explorers. Starting just below the confluence with the Green River, the gradient increases steeply, the river becoming turbulent and full of rapids for the next ninety miles until it smooths out above the ferry crossing at Hite. This section John Wesley Powell called Cataract Canyon. The cable ferry at Hite was, until construction a few years ago of the high bridge at the Glen Canyon dam site, the only point except Lee's Ferry and subsequent Navajo Bridge where the Colorado River could be crossed by automobile between Moab and Hoover Dam. At Hite, where White River Canyon enters on the left, Glen Canyon begins. It extends a winding course through the Wingate and Navajo sandstones to Lee's Ferry. Where the river emerges between the Vermilion Cliffs of the Paria Plateau and Echo Cliffs on the east, Glen Canyon ends.

—E. P.

Below the Paria the Colorado enters the older rock formation of Marble Canyon and makes the gradual transition into the renowned feature of which it is an integral part—the Grand Canyon, a place that no one yet knows well enough, but which the public as a whole rallied to protect in time. Standing beside that canyon on May 6, 1903, Theodore Roosevelt said: "In the Grand Canyon, Arizona has a natural wonder which, so far as I know, is in kind absolutely unparalleled. . . . I want to ask you to do one thing in connection with it in your own interest and in the interest of the country—to keep this great wonder of nature as it now is. . . . I hope you will not have a building of any kind, nor a summer cottage, a hotel, or anything else, to mar the wonderful grandeur, the sublimity, the great loneliness and beauty of the canyon. Leave it as it is. You cannot improve on it. The ages have been at work on it, and man can only mar it."

—D. B.

THE GLEN CANYON COMMUNITY

(*abbreviations:* r, rare; u, uncommon; o, occasional; c, common; a, abundant; T, transient; R, resident; V, visitant; ?, possible; s, summer; w, winter)

Shortly after the Colorado River Storage Project was authorized in 1956 a series of investigations was begun in areas to be affected by its proposed reservoirs. One was the salvage of archeological data in the Glen Canyon reservoir basin before its filling. Professor Robert Lister protested that survey was no substitute for excavation and pleaded for a thorough excavation program, but there was not enough time. Biological investigations were also conducted. University of Utah Anthropological Papers, No. 40, portrays the results of studies of the flora and fauna of Glen Canyon, including an ecological analysis of the vegetation, treatments of mammals, birds, reptiles, amphibians, a short list of endoparasites of rodents, an ecological study of the river, and a treatment of insects taken. Herein we abbreviate the lists of species and select a few statements from the papers in order to suggest the biological wealth that existed in the Glen Canyon Community until 1963.

"The transformation of a partly undisturbed wilderness into a reservoir," the Introduction states, "will no doubt cause drastic changes in the flora and fauna . . . The region to be affected by the Glen Canyon reservoir is one of the few remaining relatively less disturbed wilderness areas of the country where careful study may yield information about the relatively primitive biota. This may serve in assessing the impact of modern civilization, especially of the great storage reservoirs, upon the native biota."

BIRDS

western grebe (r, T)
white pelican (u, T)
double-crested cormorant (u, T)
great blue heron (c, T)
snowy egret (v, T)
black-crowned night heron (u, T)
white-faced glossy ibis (u, T)
Canada goose (c, RTs)
mallard (u, T)
pintail (u, T; Vw?)
green-winged teal (c, T; Vw?)
blue-winged teal (u, T)
cinnamon teal (u, T)
American widgeon (u, T)
shoveler (u, T)
canvasback (u, T)
lesser scaup (u, T)
common golden-eye (u, T)
turkey vulture (c, R)
Cooper's hawk (two records)
red-tailed hawk (a, R)
golden eagle (c, R)
bald eagle (r, Vw)

prairie falcon (c, R)
peregrine falcon (r, T)
pigeon hawk (r, T)
sparrow hawk (c, R)
coot (u, Rs)
killdeer (c, R)
spotted sandpiper (c, V)
California gull (u, T)
ring-billed gull (u, T)
Franklin's gull (u, T)
mourning dove (a, Rs)
great-horned owl (u, R)
spotted owl (u, R)
poor-will (c, Rs)
nighthawk (c, Rs)
white-throated swift (c, Rs)
black-chinned hummingbird (c, Rs)
broad-tailed hummingbird (c, Rs)
calliope hummingbird (u, T)
belted kingfisher (u, T)
red-shafted flicker (c, R)
yellow-bellied sapsucker (u, Vw)
western kingbird (u, Rs)
Cassin's kingbird (c, Rs)

ash-throated flycatcher (a, Rs)
Say's phoebe (c, Rs)
Traill's flycatcher (c, Rs)
western flycatcher (u, T)
western wood pewee (u, T; Rs?)
olive-sided flycatcher (u, T)
horned lark (u, R)
violet-green swallow (c, Rs)
rough-winged swallow (u, T; Rs?)
cliff swallow (c, Rs)
scrub jay (u, R)
raven (c, R)
mountain chickadee (u, Vw)
plain titmouse (u, R)
brown creeper (u, Vw)
water ouzel (u, R)
canyon wren (c, R)
rock wren (c, Rs)
mockingbird (u, R)
catbird (u, Rs)
robin (c, R)
mountain bluebird (u, T)
blue-gray gnatcatcher (c, Rs)
solitary vireo (u, T)
orange-crowned warbler (u, T)
Lucy's warbler (c, Rs)
Yellow warbler (c, Rs)
yellowthroat (c, Rs)
yellow-breasted chat (c, Rs)
yellow-headed blackbird (u, T)
red-wing (u, T; Rs?)
Bullock's oriole (c, Rs)
Brewer's blackbird (u, T)
cowbird (u, T)
western tanager (u, T)
black-headed grosbeak (u, T; Rs?)
blue grosbeak (c, Rs)
lazuli bunting (u, Rs)
linnet (c, Rs)
American goldfinch (u, R)
rufous-sided towhee (u, R)
lark sparrow (c, Rs)
black-throated sparrow (c, Rs)
sage sparrow (u, Rs)
Oregon junco (c, Wv)
chipping sparrow (c, Rs)
Brewer's sparrow (c, Rs)
white-crowned sparrow (c, Wv)
song sparrow (c, Vw)

MAMMALS

Yuma myotis
small-footed myotis
western pipistrelle
black-tailed jack rabbit
desert cottontail
rock squirrel
white-tailed antelope squirrel
Colorado chipmunk
silky pocket mouse
Apache pocket mouse
little pocket mouse
Great Basin pocket mouse
long-tailed pocket mouse
rock pocket mouse
western harvest mouse
canyon mouse
deer mouse
brush mouse
pinyon mouse
rock mouse
northern grasshopper mouse
Ord's kangaroo rat
white-throated wood rat
Mexican wood rat
desert wood rat
Stephen's wood rat
bush-tailed wood rat
beaver
porcupine
coyote
red fox
grey fox
ringtail
raccoon
long-tailed weasel
badger
spotted skunk
bobcat
mule deer
bison
mountain sheep

VEGETATION

RIVER BANK

sandbar willow
Goodding willow
baccharis
tamarisk or salt cedar
arrowweed
Gambel oak
hackberry

[168

Fremont cottonwood (r)
salt grass
slender dropseed
tall reed
wild rose (o)
squawbushes (2, o)

TERRACE VEGETATION

arrowweed
four-winged saltbush
tall inkweed
greasewood
big rabbitbrush
varnish-leaved rabbitbrush
three-lobed squawbush
narrow-leaved yucca
Harriman yucca
shadscale
Garrett saltbush
blackbrush
hedgehog cactus (2)
Opuntia cactus (2)
indigo bush (2)
water jacket
squaw thorn
matchweed
sand sage
sage (*ludoviciana*)
Fremont cottonwood
hackberry
Gambel oak
Indian rice grass
alkali sacaton

SIDE CANYON VEGETATION

Wide Canyons

sandbar willow
tamarisk
Goodding willow
Fremont cottonwood
salt grass
scratch grass
baltic rush
spike-rush (3)
sedge
horsetail
wide-leaf cattail
narrow-leaf cattail
common reed
Nuttall alkali grass
Foxtail barley
water bent grass
tule
bulrush

Narrow Canyons

Gambel oak
hackberry
boxelder

Fremont cottonwood
black chokecherry
western virgin-bower
thicket creeper
single-leaf ash
squawbush
poison sumac
wild rose
false tarragon
redbud
western horsetail
tall horsetail
Canadian wildrye
cheat grass
false solomon seal
stream orchid
vetch
cattail
liverwort
Indian hemp or dogbane

HILLSIDE VEGETATION

shadscale
cuneate salt bush
Garrett salt bush
joint-firs (2)
Indian rice grass
curly grass
water jacket
squaw thorn
indigo bush
narrow-leaved yucca
Harriman yucca
Opuntia cactus (spp.)
hedgehog cactus (spp.)
rabbitbrush
Utah service berry
hackberry
Fremont barberry
Gambel oak
hackberry
round-leafed buffalo berry
antelope brush
cliff rose
Utah service berry
single-leaf ash
single-leaf squawbush
On north-facing cliffs:
Tortula ruralis (species of moss, in blackish dense masses)
jelly lichen (Collema)
reddish brown mosses
Grimmia orbicularis, the most conspicuous moss, in large, convex, cushion tufts.
Among a general listing of herbaceous plants:
sego lily, mariposa lily, eriogonum, russian thistle,

sandwort, prickly poppy, Prince's plume, lupine, locoweed, euphorbia, globe mallow, blazing star, evening primrose, gilia, jimson weed, pentstemon, paint brush, golden aster, goldenrod, fleabane, mule ears, sunflower, gaillardia, senecio, thistle, rush pink.

VEGETATION OF SPRINGS AND SEEPS

maidenhair fern
several grasses
several columbines
red monkey flower
primrose

cardinal flower
orchid
rush
false solomon seal
willow-weed
evening primrose
speedwell
thistle
common liverwort
another liverwort
several mosses (these mosses frequently form deep and extensive tufts along wet or damp seams, and, by coalescing, may form a continuous cushion of green velvet appearance several yards in length.)

The Introduction to the paper on mammals remarks: "The procedures of the expedition were not conducive to the best production as concerns the study of mammals. The primary purpose of the expedition was to survey the vegetation . . . and all other activities were subservient to this main objective. . . . Of necessity, detailed study of the environment and preparation of adequate series of specimens was practically impossible. . . . From the data on hand, . . . the mammalian fauna of Glen Canyon consists of animals belonging to 5 orders, 3 families, 26 genera, 41 species, and 56 subspecies. It will be appreciated that this list is by no means complete." . . .

In appraising the effects of the reservoir upon mammals the paper says:

"When the reservoir becomes filled, the water, for the most part, will stand against sheer barren cliffs, slickrock, or barren desert hillsides. All habitats that currently exist in the bottom and those up to several hundred feet above the bottom will be inundated.

"We visualize that the mammalian fauna will undergo drastic changes. Beavers are doomed. Their present saturated populations will disappear because their entire area of food and den sites will be destroyed. Some may move up the tributaries, but here the food supply is scarce. Others may move upstream, if possible, into Cataract Canyon, and on into the Green and Colorado rivers. These areas, however, are already heavily populated. Deer will likewise disappear from the area largely because of the dearth of food. This may not be true of the few mountain sheep because much of their range is above the area that will be inundated. The rodents that presently inhabit the terraces, talus and hillsides will disappear because of the lack of food and home sites. Once the reservoir becomes filled, its banks will in no way provide the number and types of ecological niches which presently exist in the canyon. These banks will possibly become even more sterile because of fluctuations of the water level. Some few inhabitants of the cliffs and ledges and those who are able to live in the adjacent shallow soils may persist. For the most part, however, we believe that the mammalian fauna will become drastically reduced both in kinds and number."

The exception would be man.—D. B.

REFERENCES

[Terminal page numbers refer to the page in The Place No One Knew *upon which the material cited appears]*

BARNETT, LINCOLN. *The Universe and Dr. Einstein.* Sloane, New York, 1950. Page 120.

BERNHEIMER, CHARLES L. *Rainbow Bridge: The 1921 Expedition.* Doubleday, Page & Company, New York, 1924. Page 88.

BESTON, HENRY. *The Outermost House: A Year of Life on the Great Beach of Cape Cod.* Doubleday, Doran & Company, Inc., New York, 1929. Pages 126, 128.

BROWER, DAVID (ed.). *Wildlands in Our Civilization.* Sierra Club Bulletin, San Francisco, 1957. Page 130.

————. "The Last Days of Glen Canyon," *Sierra Club Bulletin,* 1958. Page 19.

————. *This Is the American Earth,* by Ansel Adams and Nancy Newhall. Sierra Club, San Francisco, 1960. Page 12.

————. *Wilderness: America's Living Heritage.* Sierra Club, San Francisco, 1961. Page 101.

BROWN, HARRISON. *The Challenge of Man's Future.* The Viking Press, New York, 1954, 1958. Page 148.

BURROUGHS, JOHN. (see FARIDA A. WILEY).

CHURCH, PEGGY POND. *The House at Otowi Bridge: The Story of Edith Warner and Los Alamos.* University of New Mexico Press, Albuquerque, 1962. Page 90.

DOUGLAS, WILLIAM O. *Of Men and Mountains.* Harper & Brothers, New York, 1950. Page 58.

————. *In Wilderness: America's Living Heritage.* Sierra Club, San Francisco, 1961. Pages 92, 110.

DUTTON, CLARENCE E. *The Physical Geology of the Grand Canyon District.* U.S. Geological Survey, Washington, D.C., 1882. Pages 36, 38.

————. *Tertiary History of the Grand Canyon District.* U.S. Geological Survey, Washington, D.C., 1882. Pages 32, 34, 46.

EGGERT, CHARLES. "Forbidden Passage," *Sierra Club Bulletin,* 1958. Page 76.

EINSTEIN, ALBERT (see BARNETT).

EISELEY, LOREN. *The Firmament of Time.* Atheneum, New York, 1962. Pages 50, 132, 134, 140.

————. *The Immense Journey.* Vintage Books, New York, 1946, 1957. Pages 44, 122, 136, 138, 142.

————. *The Mind As Nature.* Harper & Row, Elmsford, N. Y., 1962. Page 96.

FRUGÉ, AUGUST. in *Wilderness: America's Living Heritage.* Sierra Club, San Francisco, 1961. Page 20.

HALL, DONALD J. *Enchanted Sand.* William Morrow & Company, New York, 1933. Page 56.

HEALD, WELDON F. in *The Inverted Mountains: Canyons of the West,* Roderick Peattie (ed.). Vanguard Press, Inc., New York, 1948. Pages 86, 88, 158.

KRUTCH, JOSEPH WOOD. *Grand Canyon.* Doubleday & Company, Inc., New York, 1958. Pages 102, 144, 146.

————. *The Voice of the Desert.* William Sloane Associates, New York, 1956. Page 154.

LEOPOLD, A. STARKER. in *Wildlands in Our Civilization.* Sierra Club, San Francisco, 1957. Page 112.

LEOPOLD, ALDO. *A Sand County Almanac.* Oxford University Press, New York, 1949. Page 114.

McFARLAND, J. HORACE. White House Conference on the Conservation of Natural Resources. May 14, 1908. Page 108.

MILL, JOHN STUART. as quoted by Robert Jarrett, Resources for the Future, Washington, D.C., 1959. c. Page 124.

MUMFORD, LEWIS. *Sierra Club Bulletin,* 1962. Page 116.

PIEL, GERARD. *Science in the Cause of Man.* Alfred A. Knopf, New York, 1961. Page 104.

POPE, ALEXANDER. "An Essay on Man," *The Complete Poetical Works of Pope.* Houghton Mifflin Company, Boston, 1902. Page 98.

POWELL, JOHN WESLEY. *The Exploration of the Colorado River* (abridged). University of Chicago Press, Chicago, 1957. Pages 3, 4, 66, 68, 70, 72, 74.

ROBINSON, EDWIN ARLINGTON. *Tristram.* The Macmillan Company, New York, 1927. Page 160.

SEARS, PAUL B. in *Wilderness: America's Living Heritage.* Sierra Club, San Francisco, 1961. Page 118.

STEGNER, WALLACE. *Beyond the Hundredth Meridian: John Wesley Powell and the Second Opening of the West.* Houghton Mifflin Company, Boston, 1954. Pages 30, 40, 52, 54, 64.

————. *Mormon Country.* Duell, Sloane & Pearce, New York, 1942. Page 28.

————. "The Wilderness Idea," *Wilderness: America's Living Heritage.* Sierra Club, San Francisco, 1961. Pages 62, 150, 152, 162.

SUMNER, CID RICKETTS. *Traveler in the Wilderness.* Harper & Brothers, New York, 1957. Pages 78, 80, 82, 84.

THOREAU, HENRY DAVID. Page 94.

————. in *The Thoughts of Thoreau,* by Edwin Way Teale. Dodd, Mead & Company, New York, 1962. Page 100.

TREVELYAN, G. M. in *The Meaning of Wilderness to Science.* Sierra Club, San Francisco, 1960. Page 98.

VANDYKE, JOHN C. *The Desert: Further Studies in Natural Appearances.* Charles Scribner's Sons, New York, 1925. Page 42.

WARNER, EDITH. (see Peggy Pond Church).

WATERS, FRANK. *The Colorado.* Rinehart & Company, New York, 1946. Pages 24, 26, 156.

WEEKS, EDWARD. *In Friendly Candor.* Little, Brown & Company, Boston, 1946, 1959. Page 106.

WILEY, FARIDA A. (ed.). *John Burroughs' America: Selections from the Writings of the Hudson River Naturalist.* The Devin-Adair Company, New York, 1951. Page 48.

WISTER, OWEN. Foreword in *Through the Grand Canyon from Wyoming to Mexico,* by E. L. Kolb. The Macmillan Company, New York, 1920. Pages, 22, 60.

GLEN CANYON

GLEN CANYON DAM

PAGE

COLORADO RIVER

COTTONWOOD WASH

CROSSING OF THE FATHERS

GRAND BENCH

KAIPAROWITS PLATEAU

RAINBOW BRIDGE NATIONAL MONUMENT

RAINBOW PLAT

NAVAJO MOUNTAIN

NAVAJO PLATEAU

UTAH
ARIZONA

HOI
THE

THE WORLD OF SIDE CANYON